The ROSARY
Comic Book

Written & illustrated by
Gene Yang
Colored by Lark Pien

Includes the
Luminous Mysteries

Pauline
BOOKS & MEDIA
Boston

Published by Pauline Books & Media, 50 Saint Pauls Avenue, Boston, MA 02130-3491. www. pauline.org

Printed in the U.S.A.

TRCB KSEUSAHUDNHA1-4K48055 6479-X

Pauline Books & Media is the publishing house of the Daughters of St. Paul, an international congregation of women religious serving the Church with the communications media.

5 6 7 8 9 10 11   16 15 14 13 12

What's the Rosary?

The rosary is a prayer in which we think about, or *meditate*, on the life of Jesus. We say the rosary for the same reason we say any other prayer: to get to know Jesus, who is our Teacher, our Savior, and our Lord. Whenever we pray the rosary, Jesus' mother Mary prays with us and for us. This makes the rosary an especially powerful prayer.

When Jesus lived here on earth, people sometimes approached him with the help of his mother. Now that Mary is in heaven with Jesus, we can still bring our needs to him with her help. Praying the rosary is one of the best ways to do this.

When we pray the rosary, we remember important events in the lives of Jesus and Mary. We call these events *mysteries.* There are twenty mysteries. (It used to be the custom to think about fifteen different mysteries, but Pope John Paul II added five more not too long ago.) The twenty mysteries are separated into four groups of five mysteries each. These groups are the *joyful mysteries,* the *luminous mysteries,* the *sorrowful mysteries* and the *glorious mysteries.*

The rosary is actually made up of a series of short prayers, mainly the *Our Father,* the *Hail Mary* and the *Glory.* (You can find them all on page 6.) As we pray the rosary, we keep track of our prayers on a special chain of beads. This chain of beads is also called a *rosary*.

Before beginning your rosary, it's a great idea to talk to Jesus and Mary about all the people and things you want to pray for. Tell them about any problems or needs that you, your family or friends have. Ask them to help everyone in the world to live in peace and love. Thank Jesus and Mary for all they do for you.

How to pray it...

4. Pray the Glory. Name the Ist Mystery. Pray the Our Father.

14. Pray the Glory and the Hail, Holy Queen.

3. Pray 3 Hail Marys.

5. Pray 10 Hail Marys.

2. Pray the Our Father.

FINISH:
15. Kiss the crucifix.

6. Pray the Glory. Name the 2nd Mystery. Pray the Our Father.

START:
I. Make the Sign of the Cross, and pray the Apostles' Creed.

7. Pray 10 Hail Marys.

12. Pray the Glory.
Name the 5th Mystery.
Pray the Our Father.

13. Pray 10
Hail Marys.

11. Pray 10
Hail Marys.

8. Pray the Glory.
Name the 3rd Mystery.
Pray the Our Father.

10. Pray
the Glory.
Name the
4th Mystery.
Pray the
Our Father.

9. Pray 10 Hail Marys.

You'll need to know...

The Sign of the Cross

In the name of the Father, and of the Son, and of the Holy Spirit. Amen.

Our Father

Our Father, who art in heaven, hallowed be thy name. Thy kingdom come. Thy will be done on earth as it is in heaven. Give us this day our daily bread, and forgive us our trespasses, as we forgive those who trespass against us. And lead us not into temptation; but deliver us from evil. Amen.

Hail Mary

Hail Mary, full of grace, the Lord is with you. Blessed are you among women and blessed is the fruit of your womb, Jesus. Holy Mary, Mother of God, pray for us sinners, now and at the hour of our death. Amen.

Glory

Glory to the Father, and to the Son, and to the Holy Spirit: as it was in the beginning, is now, and will be for ever. Amen.

The Fatima Decade Prayer

O my Jesus, forgive us our sins, save us from the fires of hell. Lead all souls to heaven, especially those most in need of your mercy.

The Apostles' Creed

I believe in God, the Father almighty,
Creator of heaven and earth,

and in Jesus Christ,
his only Son, our Lord,
who was conceived by
the Holy Spirit,
born of the Virgin Mary,
suffered under Pontius Pilate,
was crucified, died and was buried;
he descended into hell;
on the third day he rose again from the dead;
he ascended into heaven,
and is seated at the right hand
of God the Father almighty;
from there he will come to judge
the living and the dead.

I believe in the Holy Spirit,
the holy catholic Church,
the communion of saints,
the forgiveness of sins,
the resurrection of the body,
and life everlasting. Amen.

Hail, Holy Queen

Hail, holy Queen, Mother of Mercy, our life, our sweetness, and our hope. To you do we cry, poor banished children of Eve; to you do we send up our sighs, mourning and weeping in this valley of tears. Turn then, most gracious advocate, your eyes of mercy toward us, and after this our exile, show unto us the blessed fruit of your womb, Jesus. O clement, O loving, O sweet Virgin Mary.

You can choose...

Your **Rosary Comic Book** tells the stories of the joyful, luminous, sorrowful and glorious mysteries of the lives of Jesus and Mary. You can use it in two ways:

1. *Read* it as you would a regular comic book.

2. *Pray* with it, using the panels in place of the beads of a traditional rosary.

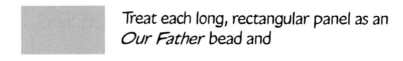 Treat each long, rectangular panel as an *Our Father* bead and

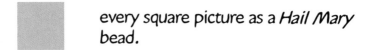 every square picture as a *Hail Mary* bead.

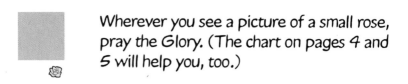 Wherever you see a picture of a small rose, pray the Glory. (The chart on pages 4 and 5 will help you, too.)

You can also read more about the mysteries of the rosary in your Bible. Just look up the verses listed at the end of each mystery.

Chapter One

The Joyful Mysteries

IN THE BEGINNING, **GOD** CREATED THE **HEAVENS** AND THE **EARTH**.

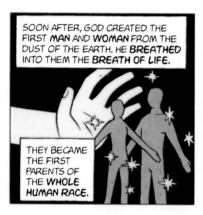

SOON AFTER, GOD CREATED THE FIRST **MAN** AND **WOMAN** FROM THE DUST OF THE EARTH. HE **BREATHED** INTO THEM THE **BREATH OF LIFE**.

THEY BECAME THE FIRST PARENTS OF THE **WHOLE HUMAN RACE**.

BUT OUR FIRST PARENTS TURNED AWA FROM **GOD'S LOVE**. THEIR DESCEND-ANTS FOLLOWED THEIR EXAMPLE, FORGETTING, OVERLOOKING, AND **REJECTING** THEIR OWN CREATOR.

YET GOD NEVER FORGOT.

GOD LONGED TO GIVE HIS OWN **DIVINE LIFE** TO THE HUMANS HE CREATED, TO **SAVE** THEM AND TO **HEAL** THEM...

The First Joyful Mystery: The Annunciation

AND SO, ONE QUIET NIGHT LONG AGO, GOD SENT THE ANGEL **GABRIEL** TO THE VILLAGE OF **NAZARETH** IN GALILEE, TO A YOUNG JEWISH WOMAN NAMED **MARY**.

REJOICE, MARY, BECAUSE THE **LORD** HAS CHOSEN YOU!

DON'T BE **FRIGHTENED!** GOD IS ABOUT TO GIVE YOU A WONDERFUL BLESSING!

SOON YOU'LL BECOME **PREGNANT** AND HAVE A BABY BOY. YOU WILL NAME HIM **JESUS**.

HE WILL BE **GREAT**, AND HE WILL BE KNOWN AS THE **SON OF THE MOST HIGH**.

HE WILL BE **KING** OF GOD'S PEOPLE FOREVER! HIS **KINGDOM** WILL NEVER END!

BUT HOW CAN I HAVE A **BABY**? MY FIANCE **JOSEPH** AND I AREN'T EVEN MARRIED YET!

THE **HOLY SPIRIT** WILL COME UPON YOU, AND THE POWER OF THE **MOST HIGH** WILL **OVERSHADOW** YOU!

Luke 1:26-38

The Second Joyful Mystery: The Visitation

IT'S JUST AS THE ANGEL SAID!

GOD HAS **BLESSED** YOU AMONG WOMEN, AND HE'S BLESSED YOUR **CHILD** AS WELL!

TO WHAT DO I OWE THIS **HONOR**, THAT THE MOTHER OF MY LORD SHOULD VISIT ME?

SHE KNOWS ALREADY?

I FELT MY BABY JUMP FOR **JOY** THE INSTANT I HEARD YOUR **VOICE**!

GOD BLESSED YOU BECAUSE YOU **TRUSTED** THAT HE WOULD KEEP HIS PROMISES.

SHE KNOWS ALREADY!

. . .

I'VE FOUND SUCH **JOY** IN GOD MY SAVIOR! HE HAS CHOSEN HIS HUMBLE **SERVANT GIRL**, AND NOW ALL FUTURE GENERATIONS WILL CALL ME **BLESSED**!

THE LORD IS **MIGHTY** AND THE LORD IS **HOLY**! HE HAS DONE **GREAT THINGS** FOR ME!

Luke 1:39-56

WHEN MARY'S FIANCE **JOSEPH** DISCOVERED THAT SHE WAS PREGNANT, HE DECIDED TO **BREAK OFF** THE ENGAGEMENT QUIETLY, SO THAT SHE WOULDN'T BE PUT TO **SHAME**.

I LOVED HER...

I LOVED HER **SO** MUCH...

BUT AS HE THOUGHT THIS OVER, JOSEPH FELL ASLEEP AND AN **ANGEL** APPEARED IN HIS DREAM.

DON'T BE **FRIGHTENED**, JOSEPH!

GO AHEAD WITH YOUR MARRIAGE TO **MARY**. THE CHILD WITHIN HER NOW WAS PUT THERE BY THE **HOLY SPIRIT**.

WHEN HE IS BORN, NAME HIM **JESUS** BECAUSE HE WILL RESCUE PEOPLE FROM **THEIR SINS**.

WHEN JOSEPH AWOKE, HE **DID** AS HE WAS TOLD.

HE BROUGHT MARY HOME TO BE HIS **WIFE**.

AT THAT TIME, THE ROMAN **EMPEROR** ORDERED THAT A CENSUS OF THE ENTIRE EMPIRE BE TAKEN. EVERYONE HAD TO GO BACK TO THEIR HOME TOWNS TO REGISTER FOR THIS CENSUS. SINCE JOSEPH WAS A DESCENDANT OF KING DAVID, HE AND MARY HAD TO GO TO **BETHLEHEM**, DAVID'S ANCIENT HOME.

WHILE THEY WERE THERE, MARY GAVE BIRTH TO HER **BABY BOY.** SHE BUNDLED HIM UP TIGHTLY IN WARM STRIPS OF CLOTH AND LAID HIM IN A **MANGER** BECAUSE THE VILLAGE INN WAS FULL.

THAT NIGHT SOME **SHEPHERDS** WERE IN THE FIELDS OUTSIDE THE VILLAGE, GUARDING THEIR FLOCKS.

DON'T **BE FRIGHTENED!** I BRING YOU GREAT NEWS!

THIS VERY NIGHT IN BETHLEHEM THE **MESSIAH** – THE SAVIOR THAT GOD PROMISED HIS PEOPLE – HAS BEEN BORN!

AND HERE'S HOW YOU WILL FIND HIM:

HE IS A BABY LYING IN A **MANGER,** BUNDLED UP TIGHTLY IN WARM STRIPS OF CLOTH.

COME ON! THAT MUST BE HIM...

...THE MESSIAH!

Matthew 1:18-25; Luke 2:1-20

MOSES' LAW REQUIRED A **PURIFICATION OFFERING** TO BE MADE AFTER THE BIRTH OF A CHILD. SO, SOME TIME AFTER JESUS WAS BORN, HIS PARENTS TOOK HIM TO **JERUSALEM** TO PRESENT HIM TO THE LORD.

IN JERUSALEM AT THE TIME THERE LIVED A MAN NAMED **SIMEON**. HE LOVED GOD WITH ALL OF HIS HEART AND PRAYED CONSTANTLY.

THE **HOLY SPIRIT** HAD TOLD HIM:

YOU WILL NOT **DIE** UNTIL YOU'VE SEEN GOD'S CHOSEN **MESSIAH**.

ON THE DAY MARY AND JOSEPH TOOK JESUS TO JERUSALEM, THE SPIRIT INSPIRED SIMEON TO GO TO THE **TEMPLE**.

MAY I...?

LORD, I CAN NOW DIE IN **PEACE**!

YOU'VE KEPT YOUR PROMISE! MY EYES HAVE SEEN THE **SAVIOR** YOU'VE GIVEN TO THE **WORLD**!

gah!

HE IS A **LIGHT** THAT WILL REVEAL **GOD** TO EVERY NATION! HE IS THE **GLORY** OF YOUR PEOPLE!

bubbub bubbub

LISTEN! MANY PEOPLE WILL REJECT THIS CHILD, BRINGING ABOUT THEIR OWN **DOWNFALL**.

BUT THROUGH HIM, MANY OTHERS WILL **RISE**.

IN THIS WAY HE WILL REVEAL THE SECRET THOUGHTS OF MANY HEARTS... AND A **SWORD** WILL PIERCE YOUR OWN **SOUL**.

Luke 2:22-35

The Fifth Joyful Mystery: The Finding of Jesus in the Temple

JESUS GREW UP HEALTHY AND STRONG IN NAZARETH OF GALILEE. GOD FILLED HIM WITH WISDOM BEYOND HIS YEARS, AND PLACED HIS SPECIAL GRACE UPON HIM.

EVERY YEAR JESUS' PARENTS WENT TO JERUSALEM FOR THE PASSOVER FESTIVAL. WHEN JESUS WAS TWELVE YEARS OLD, THEY ATTENDED THE FESTIVAL AS USUAL.

AFTER THE CELEBRATION WAS OVER, THEY HEADED HOME TO NAZARETH.

WHERE'S JESUS?

I THINK HE'S WITH YOUR COUSIN'S CHILDREN.

THAT NIGHT, JESUS WAS STILL NOWHERE TO BE FOUND. HIS PARENTS BEGAN TO SEARCH FOR HIM AMONG THEIR RELATIVES AND FRIENDS.

HAVE YOU SEEN OUR SON?

I'M SORRY, WE HAVEN'T.

WORRIED, MARY AND JOSEPH WENT BACK TO JERUSALEM TO LOOK FOR HIM THERE.

THREE DAYS PASSED BEFORE THEY FINALLY FOUND HIM.

THEREFORE, UNLESS **GOD HIMSELF** BUILDS THE HOUSE, THE WORK OF THE **BUILDERS** IS USELESS.

THIS BOY-

YES! HIS UNDERSTANDING IS **AMAZING!**

JESUS!

SON! HOW COULD YOU DO THIS TO US?

YOUR MOTHER AND I HAVE BEEN **WORRIED SICK!** WE'VE LOOKED FOR YOU **EVERYWHERE!**

BUT WHY DID YOU NEED TO SEARCH?

DIDN'T YOU KNOW THAT I WOULD BE IN MY **FATHER'S HOUSE?**

?

AFTERWARDS, JESUS WENT HOME TO NAZARETH WITH HIS PARENTS AND **OBEYED** THEM.

Luke 2:41-52

Chapter
Two

The Luminous Mysteries

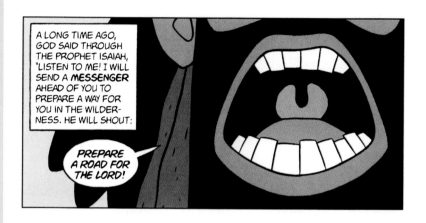

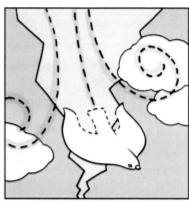

THE HOLY SPIRIT DESCENDED AS A DOVE AND CAME TO REST ON JESUS.

THIS IS MY SON, WHOM I LOVE DEEPLY. MY FAVOR RESTS ON HIM.

IMMEDIATELY JESUS WAS DRIVEN DEEP INTO THE WILDERNESS.

HE STAYED THERE FOR FORTY DAYS, BEING TEMPTED BY SATAN.

Matthew 3:13-4:1

The Second Luminous Mystery: The Wedding at Cana

SOON AFTER, JOHN THE BAPTIST WAS ARRESTED AND THROWN IN JAIL. WHEN JESUS HEARD ABOUT THIS, HE RETURNED TO GALILEE, PROCLAIMING:

THE KINGDOM OF GOD IS NEAR! TURN FROM YOUR SINS AND *BELIEVE* THIS GOOD NEWS!

AS HE WALKED ALONG THE SEA OF GALILEE, HE MET SOME OF THE LOCAL FISHERMEN.

FOLLOW ME AND I WILL MAKE YOU FISHERS OF **PEOPLE.**

THE MEN FOLLOWED JESUS AND BECAME HIS FIRST DISCIPLES.

A FEW DAYS LATER, JESUS, HIS MOTHER, AND HIS DISCIPLES ATTENDED A WEDDING CELEBRATION IN THE VILLAGE OF CANA IN GALILEE.

JESUS, THEY'VE RUN OUT OF WINE.

HOW IS THAT ANY OF OUR BUSINESS, MOTHER? MY TIME HASN'T COME YET.

John 2:1-11

26

JESUS LATER WENT BACK TO CAPERNAUM. WORD GOT AROUND THAT HE WAS THERE, AND CROWDS OF PEOPLE CAME TO SEE HIM. THE HOUSE HE WAS AT SOON BECAME SO FULL OF VISITORS THAT THERE WASN'T EVEN ROOM OUTSIDE THE DOOR. HE PREACHED THE GOOD NEWS TO THEM.

ASK AND YOU WILL RECEIVE!

SEEK AND YOU WILL FIND! KNOCK AND THE DOOR WILL BE—

?

WE'RE SORRY, TEACHER! WE COULDN'T GET TO YOU THROUGH THE CROWD.

OUR FRIEND— HE'S **PARALYZED**. WE HEARD STORIES ABOUT YOU...

MY SON, YOUR SINS ARE **FOR-GIVEN**.

27

Mark 2:1-12

The Fourth Luminous Mystery: The Transfiguration

JESUS GATHERED AROUND HIM TWELVE DISCIPLES WHO WERE MEN FROM ALL WALKS OF LIFE. HE GAVE THEM THE AUTHORITY TO CAST OUT EVIL SPIRITS AND TO HEAL ALL KINDS OF ILLNESSES. THEY BECAME HIS CLOSEST FRIENDS.

WITH THEM, JESUS CONTINUED TO TRAVEL FROM TOWN TO TOWN, PREACHING THE GOOD NEWS AND HEALING THOSE WHO CAME TO HIM.

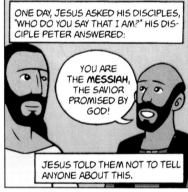

ONE DAY, JESUS ASKED HIS DISCIPLES, "WHO DO YOU SAY THAT I AM?" HIS DISCIPLE PETER ANSWERED:

YOU ARE THE **MESSIAH**, THE SAVIOR PROMISED BY GOD!

JESUS TOLD THEM NOT TO TELL ANYONE ABOUT THIS.

ABOUT A WEEK LATER JESUS TOOK PETER, JAMES, AND JOHN UP A HIGH MOUNTAIN TO PRAY.

THOSE TWO MEN WITH OUR MASTER— THAT'S **MOSES**, OUR FOREFATHER!

AND **ELIJAH** THE PROPHET!

!

MASTER, THIS IS SO **WONDERFUL!** LET'S MAKE THREE SHRINES— ONE FOR YOU, ONE FOR MOSES, AND ONE FOR ELIJAH!

RUMBLE

THIS IS MY SON, WHOM I LOVE DEEPLY. LISTEN TO HIM.

THE DISCIPLES KEPT QUIET ABOUT WHAT THEY HAD SEEN UNTIL LONG AFTER IT HAPPENED.

Mark 9:2-9

The Fifth Luminous Mystery: The Institution of the Eucharist

Matthew 26:20-29

Chapter
Three

The Sorrowful Mysteries

A FEW WEEKS BEFORE THE PASSOVER FESTIVAL, JESUS AND HIS DISCIPLES WERE VISITING THE TOWN OF BETHANY. A WOMAN APPROACHED JESUS AND POURED A VERY EXPENSIVE JAR OF OINTMENT OVER HIS HEAD.

WHY IS SHE **WASTING** THAT OINTMENT?! IT COULD HAVE BEEN SOLD AND THE **MONEY** GIVEN TO THE POOR!

LET HER DO THIS FOR ME. THE POOR WILL ALWAYS BE WITH YOU, BUT I WILL NOT. SHE IS PREPARING MY BODY FOR **BURIAL.**

SOON AFTER, JESUS' DISCIPLE JUDAS WENT TO SEE THE CHIEF PRIESTS.

HOW MUCH WILL YOU **PAY** ME IF I BETRAY MY MASTER?

THIRTY PIECES OF SILVER.

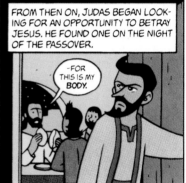

FROM THEN ON, JUDAS BEGAN LOOK-ING FOR AN OPPORTUNITY TO BETRAY JESUS. HE FOUND ONE ON THE NIGHT OF THE PASSOVER.

-FOR THIS IS MY **BODY.**

FOLLOW ME AND I'LL TAKE YOU TO HIM. THE ONE I **KISS** IS THE ONE YOU ARE TO ARREST AND TAKE AWAY.

34

The First Sorrowful Mystery: The Agony in the Garden

AFTER JESUS AND HIS DISCIPLES FINISHED THEIR PASSOVER MEAL, THEY WENT TO AN OLIVE GROVE CALLED GETHSEMANE.

MY HEART IS **BROKEN** AND MY SOUL IS **CRUSHED**. PLEASE, STAY AWAKE AND KEEP ME COMPANY.

MY FATHER! IF IT IS POSSIBLE, I BEG YOU TO TAKE THIS **SUFFERING** AWAY FROM ME!

YET I WANT YOUR WILL MORE THAN MY OWN. IF I **MUST** GO THROUGH THIS SUFFERING, THEN I WILL GO THROUGH IT.

SO YOU COULDN'T EVEN STAY AWAKE WITH ME FOR **ONE HOUR?**

WAKE UP AND STAY ALERT! PRAY THAT TEMPTATION WON'T **OVER-POWER** YOU!

LOOK, THE TIME HAS COME! MY **BETRAYER** IS HERE TO HAND ME OVER TO EVIL MEN!

TEACHER!

AS THEY **ARRESTED** JESUS, HIS DISCIPLES DESERTED HIM AND RAN AWAY.

Matthew 26:36-46

36

The Second Sorrowful Mystery: The Scourging at the Pillar

THE NEXT MORNING, THE CHIEF PRIESTS AND OTHER LEADERS TOOK JESUS TO **PILATE**, THE ROMAN GOVERNOR.

I FIND THAT THIS MAN IS INNOCENT!

BUT HE IS CAUSING **RIOTS** ALL OVER **JUDEA!**

NOW IT WAS THE GOVERNOR'S CUSTOM TO RELEASE ONE PRISONER TO THE CROWD EACH YEAR DURING THE PASSOVER CELEBRATION. AS THE CROWDS GATHERED BEFORE PILATE'S HOUSE THAT MORNING, HE ASKED THEM:

SHALL I RELEASE **BARABBAS** OR **JESUS?**

BARABBAS WAS IN PRISON FOR INSURRECTION AND **MURDER.**

BARABBAS!

WHAT, THEN, WOULD YOU HAVE ME DO WITH JESUS THE MESSIAH?

CRUCIFY HIM!

WHY? HE'S DONE NOTHING WRONG!

CRUCIFY HIM!

SO PILATE RELEASED BARABBAS...

... AND ORDERED JESUS FLOGGED WITH A **LEAD-TIPPED WHIP**, IN PREPARATION FOR CRUCIFIXION.

KRAK

NGH

Matthew 27:11-26

The Third Sorrowful Mystery: The Crowning with Thorns

Matthew 27:27-31

Luke 23:26-31

The Fifth Sorrowful Mystery: The Crucifixion

THE SOLDIERS BROUGHT JESUS TO A PLACE CALLED **GOLGOTHA**, WHICH MEANS **SKULL HILL**.

THEN THEY NAILED HIM TO THE **CROSS**.

KUNK

AAH!

TWO CRIMINALS WERE CRUCIFIED WITH HIM, ONE ON HIS RIGHT AND ONE ON HIS LEFT.

THE SOLDIERS PLAYED A GAME OF DICE TO SEE WHO WOULD GET HIS CLOTHING.

THE CHIEF PRIESTS AND OTHER LEADERS YELLED INSULTS AT HIM.

YOU SAVED OTHERS, BUT YOU CAN'T SAVE YOURSELF!

FATHER, FORGIVE THESE PEOPLE! THEY DON'T KNOW WHAT THEY'RE DOING!

AT **NOON** THE SUN WAS SUDDENLY ECLIPSED. DARKNESS COVERED THE WHOLE LAND UNTIL THREE O'CLOCK.

IT WAS THEN THAT JESUS SHOUTED,

FATHER, I ENTRUST MY SPIRIT INTO YOUR HANDS!

AND WITH THAT, HE LET OUT HIS **LAST BREATH.**

NEARBY, IN THE TEMPLE OF JERUSALEM THERE HUNG A **THICK VEIL** THAT SEPARATED THE TEMPLE'S HOLIEST INNER SANCTUM, A ROOM THAT ONLY THE CHIEF PRIESTS COULD ENTER, FROM THE REST OF THE BUILDING.

AT THE MOMENT JESUS DIED, THAT VEIL WAS **TORN APART** FROM TOP TO BOTTOM.

Luke 23:32-49

Chapter
Four

The Glorious Mysteries

SOME WOMEN WERE THERE WHEN JESUS DIED, WATCHING FROM A DISTANCE. THEY HAD BEEN HIS FOLLOWERS AND HAD CARED FOR HIM WHILE HE WAS IN GALILEE.

AMONG THEM WAS MARY MAGDALENE, THE ONE FROM WHOM JESUS HAD CAST OUT SEVEN DEMONS.

WHEN EVENING CAME, JOSEPH, A WEALTHY MAN FROM ARIMATHEA WHO HAD ALSO FOLLOWED JESUS, WENT TO SEE PILATE ABOUT JESUS' BODY.

YOU MAY TAKE IT.

JOSEPH TOOK IT AND WRAPPED IT IN A FRESH LINEN CLOTH.

JOSEPH HAD BOUGHT A TOMB FOR HIMSELF. HE PUT JESUS' BODY INSIDE OF HIS TOMB, ROLLED A LARGE ROCK ACROSS THE ENTRANCE, AND LEFT.

IT WAS FRIDAY NIGHT.

The First Glorious Mystery: The Resurrection

VERY EARLY ON SUNDAY MORNING, JUST AT SUNRISE, MARY MAGDALENE AND TWO OTHER WOMEN CAME TO THE TOMB TO PUT BURIAL SPICES ON JESUS' BODY.

WHEN THEY ARRIVED, THEY SAW THAT THE STONE HAD BEEN ROLLED ASIDE.

?!

DON'T LOOK SO SURPRISED!

YOU'RE NOT GOING TO FIND **JESUS** HERE! TOMBS ARE FOR THE DEAD, AND JESUS THE NAZARENE IS **ALIVE!**

HE HAS **RISEN** FROM THE DEAD! TAKE A LOOK AT WHERE THEY PLACED HIS BODY.

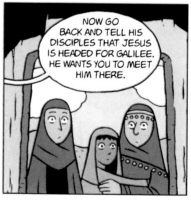

NOW GO BACK AND TELL HIS DISCIPLES THAT JESUS IS HEADED FOR GALILEE. HE WANTS YOU TO MEET HIM THERE.

THE WOMEN RUSHED BACK TO TELL JESUS' DISCIPLES WHAT HAD HAPPENED.

IMPOSSIBLE!

SOON AFTER, JESUS HIMSELF STOOD BEFORE THEM.

PEACE BE WITH YOU.

CAN I GET SOMETHING TO EAT?

THEY GAVE HIM A PIECE OF BROILED FISH AND HE ATE IT.

Luke 24:1-8, 36-43

The Second Glorious Mystery: The Ascension

DURING THE NEXT FORTY DAYS, JESUS APPEARED TO THE DISCIPLES FROM TIME TO TIME AND PROVED TO THEM IN MANY WAYS THAT HE WAS ACTUALLY ALIVE. THEN ONE AFTERNOON, HE LED THEM TO THE **MOUNT OF OLIVES**.

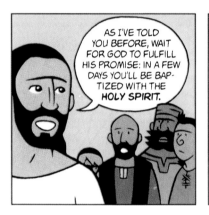

AS I'VE TOLD YOU BEFORE, WAIT FOR GOD TO FULFILL HIS PROMISE: IN A FEW DAYS YOU'LL BE BAPTIZED WITH THE **HOLY SPIRIT**.

YOU'LL RECEIVE POWER WHEN THE HOLY SPIRIT COMES DOWN ON YOU. YOU WILL TELL PEOPLE ABOUT ME EVERYWHERE—

—IN JERUSALEM, THROUGHOUT JUDEA, IN SAMARIA, AND TO ALL THE NATIONS OF THE **WORLD**!

AND KNOW THAT I WILL ALWAYS **BE WITH YOU**, EVEN TO THE END OF TIME!

Acts 1:3-14

The Third Glorious Mystery: The Descent of the Holy Spirit

ABOUT A WEEK LATER, ALL OF THE DISCIPLES MET TOGETHER IN ONE PLACE.

SUDDENLY, A LOUD NOISE CAME FROM THE SKIES. IT SOUNDED LIKE A GIANT WINDSTORM.

WHAT WAS THAT?!

EVERYBODY THERE WAS FILLED WITH THE **HOLY SPIRIT.**

MIRACULOUSLY, THEY BEGAN PRAISING GOD IN DIFFERENT LANGUAGES.

하느님, 찬양해요

¡Alabamos al Señor!

讚美主

AT THE TIME, JEWS FROM ALL OVER THE WORLD WERE IN JERUSALEM. WHEN THEY HEARD THE NOISE, THEY CAME TO SEE WHAT HAD HAPPENED.

PETER WENT OUT TO MEET THE CROWD.

LISTEN TO ME! GOD PROVED TRUE EVERYTHING JESUS SAID ABOUT HIMSELF BY WORKING WONDROUS MIRACLES AND SIGNS THROUGH HIM!

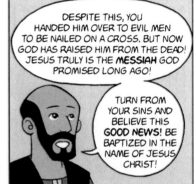

DESPITE THIS, YOU HANDED HIM OVER TO EVIL MEN TO BE NAILED ON A CROSS. BUT NOW GOD HAS RAISED HIM FROM THE DEAD! JESUS TRULY IS THE **MESSIAH** GOD PROMISED LONG AGO!

TURN FROM YOUR SINS AND BELIEVE THIS **GOOD NEWS!** BE BAPTIZED IN THE NAME OF JESUS CHRIST!

I DON'T GET IT! THESE MEN ARE FROM GALILEE...

... AND YET WE HEAR THEM SPEAKING IN THE LANGUAGES OF OUR **HOME-LANDS!**

THOSE WHO BELIEVED PETER WERE BAPTIZED AND ADDED TO THE CHURCH— ABOUT THREE THOUSAND IN ALL.

Acts 2:1-41

The Fourth Glorious Mystery: The Assumption

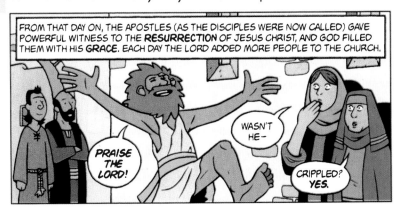

FROM THAT DAY ON, THE APOSTLES (AS THE DISCIPLES WERE NOW CALLED) GAVE POWERFUL WITNESS TO THE **RESURRECTION** OF JESUS CHRIST, AND GOD FILLED THEM WITH HIS **GRACE**. EACH DAY THE LORD ADDED MORE PEOPLE TO THE CHURCH.

PRAISE THE LORD!

WASN'T HE–

CRIPPLED? YES.

MARY THE MOTHER OF JESUS LIVED WITH THEM, OFTEN TELLING THEM OF EVENTS SHE HAD LONG TREASURED IN HER HEART.

...AND THEN HE SAID, "DIDN'T YOU KNOW THAT I WOULD BE IN MY FATHER'S HOUSE?"

EVENTUALLY THOUGH, MARY DIED.

ON THE NIGHT OF HER DEATH, IN THE QUIET OF HER TOMB, MARY RECEIVED A **VISITOR** ONCE AGAIN.

REJOICE, MARY, BECAUSE THE **LORD** REQUESTS THE PRESENCE OF YOUR BODY AND SOUL!

John 14:3

Revelation 12:1; 2 Timothy 2:11-12, 4:6-8